R

3 0 APR 2010

History in Evidence

NORMAN BRITAIN

Tony D. Triggs

Wayland

History in Evidence

Medieval Britain
Norman Britain
Prehistoric Britain
Roman Britain
Saxon Britain
Tudor Britain
Victorian Britain
Viking Britain

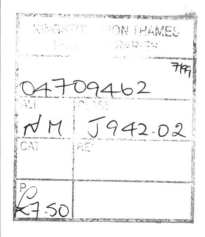
Cover design: Alison Anholt-White
Series design: Helen White
Consultant: Dr Margaret L Faull

Cover pictures: The main picture shows Restormel
Castle, in Cornwall. The inset is a stained-glass window
in Canterbury Cathedral, Kent.

First published in 1990 by
Wayland (Publishers) Limited
61 Western Road, Hove
East Sussex BN3 1JD, England

Second impression 1991

British Library Cataloguing in Publication Data
Triggs, Tony D.
    Norman Britain.
    1. Great Britain, 1066-1485
    I. Title II. Series
    942.02

HARDBACK ISBN 1-85210-579-8

PAPERBACK ISBN 0-7502-0544-X

Edited and typeset by Kudos, Hove, East Sussex
Printed in Italy by G. Canale & C.S.p.A., Turin
Bound in France by A.G.M.

Picture acknowledgements
The publishers would like to thank the following for
permission to reproduce their illustrations on the pages
mentioned: Chapel Studios Picture Library 26, 29; C M
Dixon/Photoresources *cover* (inset), 15 (upper), 20; ET
Archives 5, 9; Sonia Halliday 21 (upper); Michael
Holford 12, 15 (lower), 18, 19, 22, 25; Kudos 6; National
Trust 7 (left); Ronald Sheridan/Ancient Art & Architec-
ture Collection 27 (both), 28; Skyscan *cover* (main
picture), 16-17; TOPHAM 8, 10, 11 (both; left © Bodleian
Library), 12, 14, 15 (lower), 21 (lower), 22, 30; Tim
Woodcock 13 (both). The artwork on page 4 was
supplied by Malcolm S Walker.

Contents

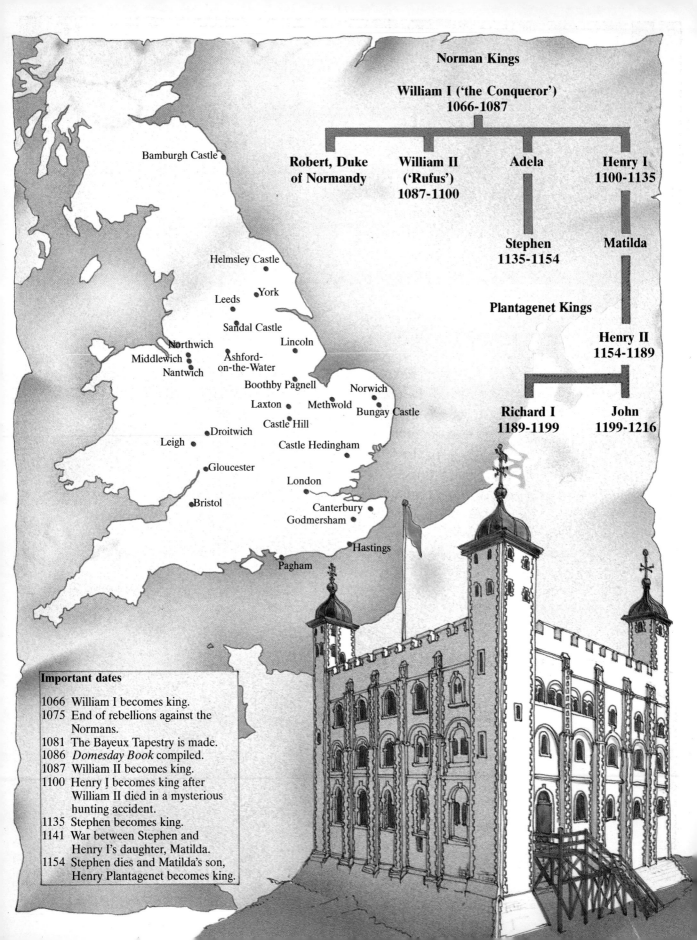

Norman Kings

William I ('the Conqueror')
1066-1087

Robert, Duke of Normandy — **William II ('Rufus') 1087-1100** — **Adela** — **Henry I 1100-1135**

Stephen 1135-1154 — **Matilda**

Plantagenet Kings

Henry II 1154-1189

Richard I 1189-1199 — **John 1199-1216**

Bamburgh Castle

Helmsley Castle

Leeds • York

Sandal Castle

Northwich • Lincoln

Middlewich • Ashford-on-the-Water

Nantwich

Boothby Pagnell

Laxton • Methwold • Norwich

Castle Hill • Bungay Castle

Droitwich

Leigh • Castle Hedingham

Gloucester • London

Bristol • Canterbury

Godmersham

Hastings

Pagham

Important dates

1066 William I becomes king.
1075 End of rebellions against the Normans.
1081 The Bayeux Tapestry is made.
1086 *Domesday Book* compiled.
1087 William II becomes king.
1100 Henry I becomes king after William II died in a mysterious hunting accident.
1135 Stephen becomes king.
1141 War between Stephen and Henry I's daughter, Matilda.
1154 Stephen dies and Matilda's son, Henry Plantagenet becomes king.

Who were the Normans?

The Normans were the people who ruled much of northern France in the tenth and eleventh centuries. They had come from the Viking lands of the north (in modern-day Scandinavia), and their name means 'North Men'. The part of France they ruled is known as Normandy, and their leader in the middle of the eleventh century was known as Duke William, or William of Normandy.

At that time, England was ruled by King Edward the Confessor. Edward had grown up in Normandy; he knew Duke William and he may have encouraged him to be the next king of England. However, Edward had an English wife, and her brother, Harold, also wanted to be the next king. Edward died in 1066 and Harold was crowned, but William brought an army over to England and defeated the English in the Battle of Hastings. Harold died in the Battle and William took his place as king.

He ruled until 1087 and is usually known as William the Conqueror, or William I. He was followed by his sons William II and Henry I, and then by his grandson, Stephen. The next king of England, Henry II, was not a Norman. His father was a French noble called Geoffrey Plantagenet,

This page from a Norman book shows Kings William I and II (top), Henry I and Stephen.

so Henry II and his sons formed a new line of kings, called the Plantagenets.

During the reign of William I, a group of women embroidered a huge comic-strip, called the Bayeux Tapestry. Its pictures give us clues about clothes, weapons, buildings and food during Norman times. The Tapestry is on display at Bayeux, in France, and copies of it can be seen in English museums.

OPPOSITE All the places mentioned in this book are shown here. The picture shows William I's White Tower, in London.

The feudal system

After his victory at Hastings, William felt that he could do what he liked with England. However, about 25 per cent of the land had belonged to the Church, and William allowed the Church to keep it. He kept the same amount for himself, and he shared what was left among his barons. He gave each baron estates in various

ABOVE In order to prove that William the Conqueror had given him a piece of land, a Norman baron would have received a document like this one. It was called a land charter.

OPPOSITE A village once surrounded this Norman church at Shoreham in East Sussex.

parts of the country. Giving each baron scattered estates was very wise. If he had given each baron a single, huge estate, some of them might have grown too powerful – and tried to take more. In return for their land, the barons had to fight for the king if trouble arose. They also had to provide extra knights if they were needed. The system of giving out land and duties, with each man having a master above him, is known as feudalism.

Because they had received their land from William, the barons were known as his tenants-in-chief. However, they shared their land out, just as William had done, and their tenants had to share the duty of fighting or providing knights for their king in time of war.

The tenant in charge of a village was usually known as the lord of the manor, because 'manor' was the name given to his mansion and the farmland around it. The villagers farmed the fields to provide their own food, but they also had to do some work for the lord of the manor, and they might have to pay him rent or give him some of their produce. An old document shows that at Pagham, in West Sussex, they had to give him one fattened pig out of every six they owned.

Most manor houses had a barn where the villagers took the produce they owed to their lord. A few Norman barns and manor houses can still be seen. There is a stone manor house at Boothby Pagnell, in Lincolnshire (see page 13), and a wooden one at Godmersham, in Kent, which the Normans turned into a barn.

`Domesday Book`

For hundreds of years, monks in England had recorded the most important events in a book called the *Saxon Chronicle*. Printed copies can be seen in libraries, and according to the entry for 1085, *'at Gloucester at midwinter . . . King William had deep speech with his counsellors. Then he sent men all over England to find out how much land and livestock each landowner held . . . and what it was worth.'*

William's officials interviewed a wide range of people, from barons to poor villagers, and one official noted down the questions which he had to ask. He had to find out:

1. The name and size of a place and who owned it;
2. The number of ploughs (or oxen to pull them);
3. The number of freemen (who owned some land) and slaves (with no land);
4. The amount of woodland, meadow and pasture;
5. The number of mills and fishponds;
6. The changes which had taken place since 1066.

Domesday Book **can be seen at the Public Records Office in London. After *Domesday Book* had been completed, William I knew nearly everything there was to be known about his kingdom.**

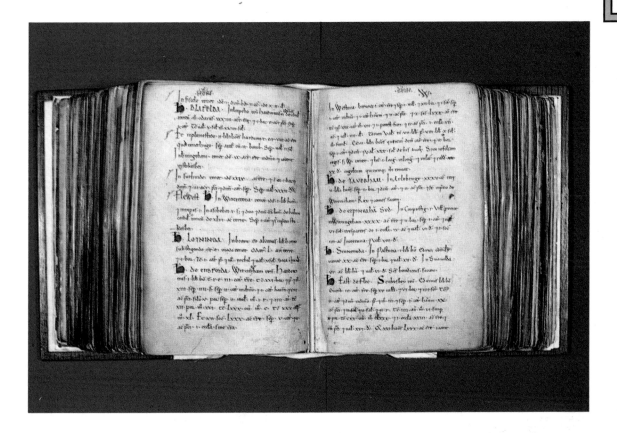

Here is a close-up of two pages of *Domesday Book*. They are written in Latin, but all the information has now been translated. Your local library will be able to tell you where you can see *Domesday Book*'s description of your county.

When the survey was finished, Norman scribes copied most of the information out neatly. Then they bound their work together in strong covers. The work is known as *Domesday* (or *Domesday Book*) because *dome* was an English word meaning judgement. People believed that God would judge them after death, sending some of them to Heaven and some to hell. They felt that William was judging them too, and they feared that *Domesday Book* would help him to charge them heavier taxes in future years.

Domesday Book was written in Latin but many libraries have translations, and it is easy to look up the entries for your town or village. The *Book* shows all sorts of interesting details. For example, it shows that many manors in northern England had fallen in value; this was due to the savage, destructive way in which William's soldiers had crushed rebellions. Some parts of the north are not included in the *Book*, since William was still having trouble in keeping the people who lived there under his control.

Farming

ABOVE The village of Laxton, in Nottinghamshire, where large fields are still divided into strips for farming as they were in Norman times.

Most villages had some very large fields where crops could be grown and animals grazed. The villagers usually worked together to do the difficult job of ploughing. Old pictures show how a simple wooden plough was pulled by a pair of oxen. The oxen had to be guided, and sometimes poked to make them move!

The fields consisted of strips of land which were shared out among the various families. The fields were large, and the soil was sometimes fertile in one place and poor in another. Each family had a number of separate strips in each field, since this ensured that everyone had an equal share of the poorer soil as well

as the better soil.

In one field, the villagers used their strips to grow a grain crop, like oats or wheat. In another field, they grew more grain, or maybe a crop like peas or beans. Finally, there was a field where they let weeds and grass spring up. They grazed their cattle and sheep in this field, and the animals' dung helped to make the soil richer. Then, in the following year, they used this field for one of their crops and a different field was used for the animals. By changing the fields from year to year, the villagers kept them in good condition.

The village had some common (or shared) land for grazing animals and growing hay. Most villages also had some woodland. The villagers went there for firewood and timber and they let their pigs grow fat on the acorns. Wood was important for making all sorts of every-day items, like dishes, buckets and bowls.

As well as the villagers' homes (which were little more than huts), most villages had a church and perhaps a water-mill for grinding corn. The largest building of all was the house where the lord of the manor lived with his family. The lord had some farmland of his own, and the villagers often had to leave their strips to work in his fields.

We know about Norman village life from very old maps and documents. There are also places where we can still see signs of the villagers' strips. The pattern

Pictures like these ones above show us the tools and clothes of Norman farmers.

ABOVE This picture shows how a farmer sowed seeds in Norman times.

shows up in modern fields, especially in photographs taken from the air. Lastly, there are one or two places where the land is still farmed in strips. The best example of this is at Laxton, in Nottinghamshire.

In the north of England, farming methods were often different, with separate families looking after the land around their homes. In the Yorkshire Dales, you can still see the pattern of scattered farms. The buildings have usually been rebuilt, but they often stand on Norman sites.

Houses

In Norman times, there were various types of house, depending on how rich the owner was. The poorest people took very tall poles and pushed them into the ground in two rows. The rows sloped towards each other so that they met at the tops. Other poles were added to make the framework strong; then the spaces were filled in with sticks which were woven together like basketwork. Finally, the owner finished off the hut by adding a roof made of thatch.

Better-off people had cruck-built homes. This meant they took whole trees and they split the trunks into sturdy posts, one for each corner of the house. They tried to use wood which curved naturally, so that when they set the posts in the ground, the tips of each pair would meet at the highest point of the house. After adding other posts and beams, they finished the walls with woven sticks and a coating of clay (usually known as wattle and daub); then they thatched the roof.

This scene from the Bayeux Tapestry shows Harold and some friends enjoying a meal in a house with two floors. The building on the left of the house is a church.

These two photographs show the inside and outside of the manor house at Boothby Pagnell.

NORMAN HOUSES

We know about the houses in Norman England in various ways. Some cruck-built ones can still be seen, though later owners have usually filled in the walls with bricks. We can also study old drawings and pictures. The Bayeux Tapestry shows a two-storey house which was built of stone. This sort of house was finer than a cruck-built house, and most were probably manor houses. A few examples still exist, including the one at Boothby Pagnell, in Lincolnshire. People probably lived on the top floor, while the ground floor was used as a storeroom or an animal shed. (Animals would have helped to keep the people warm.)

Castles

ABOVE The strong walls of Bamburgh Castle, in Northumberland.

As the Normans conquered England, they built castles. Their soldiers used them as bases and as places to shelter when the English attacked them.

In the early years, the Normans built simple castles. They would dig a circular ditch, piling up the soil from it to make a mound in the centre. They levelled the top of the mound and put a strong fence around it. Then they built a wooden tower and perhaps some other buildings on top of the mound. The Normans knew that attackers would find it very hard to cross

LIFE AT SANDAL CASTLE

At Sandal Castle, near Wakefield in Yorkshire, archaeologists have found all sorts of clues about the work which had to be done. For example, they have found fire-blackened stone from ovens which were built in the open air. They have also found forges, workshops and stables.

Old documents in Leeds City Archives also give clues about life in this castle. For example, we know that in one year Sandal Castle used grease from 67 dead pigs to oil its equipment. The equipment included a crane which was needed for raising timber to the top of the mound.

The motte (mound of earth) and remains of the keep of Helmsley Castle, Yorkshire.

the ditch and climb up the mound, especially under a hail of arrows and other objects!

Often there was not enough room at the top of the mound to house all the soldiers, so the Normans began to make their castles bigger by adding an extra loop of ditch. The space inside it was known as the 'bailey'. In times of danger, all the soldiers took up positions on top of the mound. A Norman mound and ditches can still be seen at Castle Hill in Leicestershire, but the wooden buildings have disappeared.

In many cases, the Norman barons replaced the wooden buildings of the first castles with stone ones. (Sometimes, they built in stone from the start.) Thus, a high stone wall was built around the top of a mound instead of a wooden fence. Some of these walls included towers, and some were really the outside walls of a ring of stone buildings.

Huge stone castles were built in cities like Lincoln, Norwich, York and London. *Domesday Book* sometimes mentions these castles; it also shows how badly the Normans treated the English. For example, it says that a large part of York was destroyed when the Normans built their castle, while hundreds of people lost their homes in Norwich and Lincoln. The castle in Norwich still overlooks the city centre, and part of the moat around it is now a park.

The main building in a Norman castle was called the 'keep'. Large stone keeps could not be built on mounds, since the earth would crumble under their weight. So, the Normans chose natural hills. Soil from the ditch was piled around the base of the keep, so attackers still had a difficult and dangerous climb.

This section of the Bayeux Tapestry shows Norman soldiers building a castle at Hastings.

Life in a castle

Most of the men who guarded a castle were doing a few days' military service before returning to their homes. While on duty, they lived in the castle's bailey. The keep was the home of the baron, his family and most of their staff or followers. The most important part of the keep was a massive room called the great hall. Most great halls were cold and dismal, in spite of having a log fire in a central hearth. The fire produced more smoke than heat. It drifted above the people's heads, blackening walls and curling around the beams of the roof before escaping from tiny windows.

Chunks of meat were probably roasted over the fire. However, most of the food was prepared in kitchens and brought to the hall by maids and servants, who had to climb a spiral staircase in one of the corners. The baron and his family ate at a trestle table on a low platform, and they often had a canopy (a special low ceiling) above their heads, which protected them from the draughts and smoke. In some Norman buildings, such as Thornhill Lees Hall, in Yorkshire, archaeologists have picked out the places where the canopy was fixed to the walls. The canopy and the platform showed the baron's importance; so did his silver bowls and cups. All the other people in the castle ate at tables round the sides of the hall, and if they had any tableware, it was probably made of pottery or wood.

Behind the baron's platform there was a curtain or screen to hide his bed. Everyone else had to sleep on the stone floor,

using bags or heaps of straw for comfort and rugs or cloaks to keep out the cold.

A castle employed a wide range of workers. For example, there were smiths and carpenters to keep all the weapons in good repair and grooms to look after the horses that were kept in the bailey. There were priests to say prayers and scribes to write letters and documents. A steward checked on the huge stocks of food and the brewing of ale. He also ensured that the cooks, servants and laundry-women worked as hard as possible. Lastly, the steward made sure that plenty of candles were being prepared to keep the stairways lit in winter.

Workshops and living quarters are shown in this picture of Restormel Castle, Cornwall.

Warfare

Warfare affected all kinds of people under the Normans. Sometimes the very poor had to leave their fields and fight; or they might be the victims of raids in which their homes were destroyed and their crops were trampled by horses' hoofs. Barons were sometimes trapped in their castles for many months, and kings often risked their lives in battle.

The commonest weapons were bows and arrows. Under the Normans, a new sort of bow was introduced. Known as the crossbow, it fired the arrows with much more power than the old sort of bow. They sometimes pierced the chainmail soldiers wore for protection. However, the cross-

This part of the Bayeux Tapestry shows the Normans (on horses) attacking the English at Hastings. Notice that both sides wore the same sort of armour, which was made of chainmail (small links of metal). Soldiers carried large shields, heavy swords, spears and even axes.

bow was heavy, clumsy and hard to use, so it never replaced the older longbow.

Most men went into battle on foot. They needed both hands for their bows and arrows, so they rarely had shields or other weapons. Those with axes, spears or swords carried shields as well, and they sometimes went into battle on horseback. They could ride at the enemy lines and try to break them up, but they had to beware of the pikes which were used to make a sort of fence. The 'fence' sloped outwards towards the attackers, piercing the body of any horse which galloped into it.

A battle was usually over in a single day, but it might take months to capture a castle. The keep was built very strongly; the soldiers inside could fire their arrows from the narrow windows and also from the battlements. Rocks or boiling-hot liquid were dropped on any attackers who managed to cross the moat and climb up the sloping bank.

Attackers might have to wait until the defenders ran out of food and gave up; or they might be able to poison the castle's water supply if they found the right streams. In any case, there was always the chance that disease and sickness would break out due to the filthy, overcrowded conditions inside the castle.

Sometimes attackers tried to damage the castle walls by hurling rocks from catapults. They also tried to bring the walls down by digging tunnels underneath them. While they were working, they held up the roof of their tunnel with tree-trunks. Then they set the trunks on

ABOVE This is the Norman keep at Castle Hedingham, in Essex.

fire and escaped from the tunnel. They hoped to see part of the castle collapse as the trunks burned through. We can still see the remains of a tunnel at Bungay Castle, in Suffolk.

Attackers sometimes tried to fill part of the moat so that they could cross it easily. As they worked, they sheltered under a special shield, which was known as a tortoise. Once the job was done, they could charge at the castle with a battering ram. Sometimes they also had towers, which they could wheel into place against the walls, or ladders, which they could place against them. Some men reached the battlements, but most were killed.

Monasteries and churches

Here is a close-up of some of the beautiful Norman carvings on the side of the stone font (the basin for holding water for christenings) in the church at Portchester, in Hampshire.

Many English churches and monastery buildings were small and plain, but the Normans brought a new style of building. They built new churches all over the country, and these were often very grand, with all sorts of carvings and decorations.

Nowadays, many Norman churches seem rather gloomy, and some people feel that the pillars and arches are too thick and heavy. When they were built, a lot of the churches had colourful wall-paintings, but these have faded and disappeared. However, York Minster still has some fine, gleaming stained-glass windows made by some Norman artists.

The paintings and windows showed scenes from the Bible. Few people could read, so the scenes were a way of telling them what the Bible said.

Monasteries were places where groups of monks or nuns lived and prayed. The monastery church was the largest building, but there were also buildings where the monks or nuns slept and an infirmary where they went for treatment if they were ill. There were kitchens, dining-rooms and workshops, as well as rooms for travellers, beggars and others in need. Monasteries were the only places where people could go for shelter or nursing.

ABOVE **This colourful stained-glass window can be seen in York Minster.**

also received a lot of gifts. As a result, the monks and nuns began to live a life of ease, neglecting their duties of prayer and hard work. To deal with this problem, new monasteries were sometimes started with harsher sets of rules. In 1098, a group of monks built a new monastery at Cîteaux, in France. They were known as Cistercians and their rules were adopted in other places. For example, Cistercian monasteries were founded at Rievaulx, Kirkstall and Fountains in Yorkshire, and their ruined buildings can still be seen.

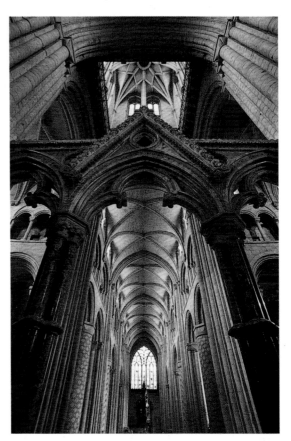

This is the inside of Durham Cathedral which was once the church of a monastery.

The monks or nuns had to live according to very strict rules, and larger libraries may have copies of these which you can read. Often, the monks or nuns had to get up at 2 a.m.; then there were prayers every two or three hours from dawn to dusk. The monks or nuns had to eat in silence; they also had to copy out parts of the Bible or work in the monastery gardens. One young monk said in a letter home that all he had for a pillow was a holy book.

The monasteries had to grow their own food, but they sometimes owned more land than they needed. They often made money by selling their produce, and they

Food and drink

We know quite a lot about what the Normans ate and drank. Some clues come from *Domesday Book*. For example, it mentions manors with vineyards, including one in Wiltshire which produced many barrels of wine each year. It also mentions a place called Methwold, in Norfolk, which had 27 beehives. The bees were kept for their honey, and this reminds us that honey was all the Normans had to sweeten their food.

The Normans also used salt. This was obtained by putting salty water in pans and letting the water evaporate, leaving the salt behind. Salt, like honey, was more important than it is today. Adding salt was the only way in which people could keep meat from going bad.

Domesday Book mentions places where fish and eels were caught. It also tells us that cattle, sheep and pigs were kept in many villages. The cattle were kept for

ABOVE This section of the Bayeux Tapestry shows a royal banquet taking place.

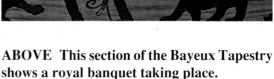

SALT WORKS
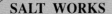
We know where the Normans made salt since 'wich' in a place name usually refers to a very old salt works. So Droitwich in Worcestershire and Northwich, Middlewich and Nantwich in Cheshire were all places where there were salt works.

their meat and milk. Some of the milk was drunk and the rest was made into butter and cheese. (The cattle's hide, or leather, was used to make things like bottles, belts, shoes and harnesses.) The pigs and sheep were also eaten, though large flocks of sheep were kept for their wool, which was made into cloth.

The king and his favourites went

hIC:COQVI TVR:CARO ET hIC: MINISTRAVERVN MINISTRI

This part of the Bayeux Tapestry shows servants preparing a meal for Duke William just before the Battle of Hastings. The food is being cooked over an open fire, away from a house.

hunting in the royal forests, and were able to feast on boar and venison. Poorer people could not do this – they were likely to have their hands cut off if they dared to hunt in these forests. However, they sometimes caught pigeons and other birds to add to their diets. They also picked nuts and berries.

Villagers had small vegetable gardens, where they grew herbs and cabbages. They used them, along with barley, peas or beans from the fields, to make soup. Sometimes they added a little stewed meat, but often there was none to spare. However, they did have lots of oats. We still use one of the Norman words for oats when we speak of a 'haversack' (which used to be a bag for carrying oats) or a 'havercake' (which is made with oats). We know where large amounts of oats were grown from place names – Haver-croft, in Yorkshire, for instance.

There were wheat fields near most villages. The local miller ground the wheat into flour, and the villagers used it to make themselves bread. Bread was a major part of their diets. As well as eating lumps of bread, the villagers sometimes put it into a bowl and poured their steaming-hot soup or stew on top.

Pastimes

In the 1100s, a Londoner wrote that the city's young men *'exercised in leaping . . . wrestling, casting of stones and throwing of javelins.'* In winter they also skated on the river Thames which often froze over.

Some of their pastimes helped to keep men trained for battle. Target practice with bows and arrows was very important, and richer people held jousting tournaments. They rode at each other with lances and tried to knock each other on to the ground. Some contestants were killed, and in the end new forms of jousting were introduced. For example, competitors tilted (or aimed their lances) at a board or ring. Sometimes the board was fixed to an arm which could swing round and knock the man off. It was safer to be knocked off like this than by a lance.

Music was a very important form of entertainment. Most people could play an instrument, though the poor had to manage with whistles which they made for themselves from sticks or bones. Early forms of the flute, horn, guitar and violin were also very popular, and a drummer beat out a regular rhythm while other people played or sang. We can still read the words of some of their songs. Many were like hymns, but others told of love, brave deeds and the coming of summer. One of the songs is still sung today. It is called 'Sumer is icumen in' (Summer has

arrived) and it praises the cuckoo for its joyful sound.

Most of the singers were wandering minstrels. They often found work in rich people's homes, since a good day's hunting was usually followed by feasting and music. Rich people also liked dancing – especially if they were not too full. Poorer people like dancing too, but only the wealthy could afford musicians in their homes. However, there were probably entertainers who did their acts on village greens for a handful of coins or some food or ale. These included jugglers, acrobats and people with performing bears. There were also groups of wandering actors. The plays they performed were usually based on Bible stories. Like the pictures in churches, these were a way of teaching people who could not read.

In quieter moments, people played board-games, like draughts and backgammon. We know about these from pictures and also from playing pieces which have been found. Chess was extremely popular. Even during the long winter evenings, life was rarely dull.

OPPOSITE Hunting with hawks and dogs was a favourite pastime of Norman barons and their friends, as this part of the Bayeux Tapestry shows. The forests were full of boar, wolves, deer and foxes for the barons to catch.

Towns

ABOVE Here are the remains of a Norman wall in the city of Lincoln.

Central and southern England had a number of thriving towns when the Normans arrived. Like York in the north, they were trading centres. For centuries, merchants had had to pay a toll when they entered a town to sell their goods. This toll had always gone to the king or his officials, and William I continued to

TRADE TOLLS
Many old documents give us clues about the tolls. For example, we read that the merchants of the city of Bristol bought the right to trade 'throughout the whole of England, Normandy and Wales' without paying any tolls at all. It is clear from this that other traders had to pay tolls wherever they went.

collect the tolls from ancient towns, such as Lincoln and Chester.

Many of William's barons wanted to start new towns and collect their own tolls. First, they needed the king's permission to set up a market or fair where traders could meet to do business. Once this was granted, the town could be built. Some wealthy barons planned their own towns and organized the building work; in other towns, people built houses and workshops to suit themselves. The presence of a castle or monastery helped a town to succeed, since the people who lived there needed workers. They also needed to buy supplies from local traders.

Domesday Book shows that towns were generally very small. Even ancient towns had only about 500 houses. However, most towns had sturdy walls to protect

ABOVE This Norman gate-house can be seen today in Canterbury, in Kent.

ABOVE The Normans left their mark on the city of York.

them, and these left little space for new building. As a result, most towns became extremely crowded. The gloomy alleys buzzed with flies, for rubbish was simply thrown out to rot. To make matters worse, the houses did not have proper toilets: some people tipped their slops into the gutters; others used a hole in the soil behind their homes. There was no running water, and people had to get their supplies from wells or pools. The water was often full of dirt and wriggling insects, and many people caught diseases.

Trade

In the eleventh and twelfth centuries, most of the workers in towns were traders, craftsmen and their assistants. Most of the alleys were lined with shops, above which their owners usually lived.

Names like Baker Street and Pudding Lane remind us that in many streets all the people did the same sort of work. This was partly because each trade was looked after by a different guild or society. Everyone in the street paid the guild a fee each year and it made sure that outsiders could not enter the town and take away its members' business by doing the same sort of work themselves. In some cases, local traders were also protected by law. For example, a royal document has survived which tells us that merchants visiting Bristol had to buy hides, corn and wood from the townspeople and not from outsiders. Guilds also checked on the quality of work and on the training of apprentices, and they helped any members who were having problems.

These coins were made in William I's reign (his head is on the left one). They were made of silver.

This house in Lincoln, which is called the Jew's House, is one of the few remaining Norman houses in England. The rounded arches above the door and the windows tell us it is Norman.

There were guilds for saddlers, carpenters, smiths and other craftsmen, as well as for those who prepared and sold food.

Many buildings were made of wood and they often caught fire, especially in streets with bakeries. However, some of the most important buildings were made of stone. These included the homes of wealthy merchants who traded with foreign countries. For centuries, English woollen cloth had been sent all over Europe. Lincoln was a centre for some of this trade; it was famous for its cloth dyed in strong red and green colours. (Even today people speak of 'Lincoln green'.) Lincoln has two fine stone-built houses from the time of the Norman kings. They probably belonged to merchants who had made themselves rich by exporting cloth. Lincoln also has a guildhall dating from Norman times. This was where the members of one of the guilds used to hold their meetings.

As well as sending cloth abroad, the merchants used to import all sorts of foreign goods. Silk, gems, spices, wine, oil, glass and ivory were among the things they brought into the country.

Places to visit

Bamburgh, Northumberland: castle
Boothby Pagnell, Lincolnshire: manor house
Buildwas, Shropshire: monastery's remains
Bungay, Suffolk: castle
Canterbury, Kent: cathedral and Eastbridge hospital
Castle Acre, Norfolk: castle, priory and town remains
Castle Rising, Norfolk: castle and church
Dalmeny, Lothian: church
Dunfermline, Fife: church
Durham: castle and cathedral
Ely, Cambridgeshire: cathedral
Fountains, North Yorkshire: monastery's remains
Heath, Shropshire: deserted village and chapel
Inverurie, Grampian: castle
Leuchars, Fife: church
Lincoln: cathedral and houses
London: British Museum, Museum of London, Tower of London, Victoria and Albert Museum
Lumphanan, Grampian: castle site
Much Wenlock, Shropshire: castle site
Norwich, Norfolk: castle, cathedral and 'Music House', King Street
Old Sarum, Wiltshire: castle and cathedral site
Pembroke, Dyfed: castle

Reading, Berkshire: the museum sometimes has a copy of the Bayeux Tapestry on display
Rievaulx, North Yorkshire: monastery's remains
St Davids, Dyfed: cathedral
Southampton, Hampshire: houses, town wall
Tyninghame, Lothian: church

Young Archaeologists Club
If you are interested in finding out more about archaeology, you might like to join this club: Young Archaeologists Club, United House, Piccadilly, York PO1 1PQ.

BELOW This leather shoe has survived since Norman times. It probably belonged to a rich person, perhaps a baron.

Glossary

Ale Strong beer.

Baron A powerful Norman nobleman who owned many manors (*see below*).

Battlement The walkway along the top of a castle's walls.

Boar A large, wild pig.

Dismal Gloomy.

Embroider Use a needle and thread to decorate a piece of material with designs or pictures.

Estate Another name for a 'manor' (*see below*).

Evaporate To heat a liquid up so that it 'disappears' into a gas.

Fertile This is usually used to describe soil which is good for growing crops.

Forge A workshop where things are made out of metal.

Harsh Cruel.

Hearth A fireplace.

Import To bring in goods from another country.

Interview To meet someone so that you can ask them questions.

Manor A large house and its land.

Merchant A business person.

Neglect To forget about doing something.

Pike A long spear.

Rebellion Fighting a person or people who are ruling over you.

Savage Cruel.

Scribe An old name for someone whose job was to write things out.

Shelter A place where you are protected from the weather or your enemies.

Sturdy Strong.

Tapestry A piece of embroidered cloth for hanging on a wall.

Thriving Growing quickly.

Toll Money paid so that you can use or do something.

Trestle table A simple table made with a wooden board laid across two supports.

Venison Meat from deer.

Books to read

Burke, J. *The Castle in Medieval England* (Batsford, 1978)

Denny, N. & Filmer-Sankey, J. *The Bayeux Tapestry* (Collins, 1966)

Hallam, E. *Domesday Heritage* (Arrow, 1986)

Kerr, N. & M. *A Guide to Norman Sites in Britain* (Granada, 1984)

Lane, P. *Norman England* (Batsford, 1980)

Nichol, J. *The Normans* (Blackwell, 1980)

Rooke, P. *The Normans* (Macdonald, 1981)

Unstead, R. J. *Kings, Barons and Serfs* (Macdonald, 1971)

Yeatman, L. *The Normans in Europe* (Chambers, 1976)

Index